You're never too old to...

YOU'RE NEVER TOO OLD TO...

Copyright © Summersdale Publishers Ltd, 2011

All rights reserved.

No part of this book may be reproduced by any means, nor transmitted, nor translated into a machine language, without the written permission of the publishers.

Condition of Sale
This book is sold subject to the condition that it shall not, by way of trade or otherwise, be lent, re-sold, hired out or otherwise circulated in any form of binding or cover other than that in which it is published and without a similar condition including this condition being imposed on the subsequent publisher.

Summersdale Publishers Ltd
46 West Street
Chichester
West Sussex
PO19 1RP
UK

www.summersdale.com

Printed and bound in the Czech Republic

ISBN: 978-1-84953-196-2

All images © Shutterstock

Substantial discounts on bulk quantities of Summersdale books are available to corporations, professional associations and other organisations. For details telephone Summersdale Publishers on (+44-1243-771107), fax (+44-1243-786300) or email (nicky@summersdale.com).

To: ....

From: ....

You're never too old to…

You're never too old to...

... eat all the chocolate off your biscuit first.

You're never too old to...

... fall in love.

You're never too old to...

... feed the ducks.

You're never too old to…

… write letters to your heroes about why you admire them.

You're never too old to...

... wear sequins.

You're never too old to…

… dance all night – or at least until the neighbours start to complain!

You're never too old to...

... surf the internet.

You're never too old to...

... start with dessert, move on to the main course and finish with a starter.

You're never too old to...

... be called 'young man' or 'young lady' by *somebody*.

You're never too old to...

... try a new sport,
like sky-diving.

You're never too old to...

... tickle a dog's tummy.

You're never too old to...

... learn something silly, like backwards writing.

You're never too old to...

... try a new type of cheese.

You're never too old to...

... give an unexpected present to a friend.

You're never too old to...

... go to see the
penguins at the zoo.

You're never too old to...

... do a striptease.

You're never too old to...

... act like a teenager.

You're never too old to...

... be confused.

You're never too old to...

... eat another piece of cake.

You're never too old to...

... meet the person of
your dreams – every day,
when you wake up.

You're never too old to...

... take up yoga.

You're never too old to...

... dance the tango.

You're never too old to...

... prefer diamonds.

You're never too old to...

... be a master of the air guitar.

You're never too old to...

... go inside the Great Pyramid.

You're never too old to...

... throw a party.

You're never too old to...

... write a best-seller.

You're never too old to...

... do something daring.

You're never too old to...

... wear red socks.

You're never too old to...

... plant a tree and
dedicate it to someone.

You're never too old to...

... ride a tandem.

You're never too old to...

... make silly faces at people when they're not looking.

You're never too old to...

... lie under a big tree (blankets are allowed) and spend an hour just gazing up at the branches.

You're never too old to...

... consider roller skates
as a mode of transport.

You're never too old to...

... watch the waves
rolling into shore.

You're never too old to...

... touch an iceberg.

You're never too old to...

... make it a double.

You're never too old to...

... give someone flowers.

You're never too old to...

... get on the next train
out of town and get off
somewhere new.

You're never too old to...

... laugh. Think about something that made you laugh and giggle all over again.

You're never too old to...

... win the Lottery. How would you spend your loot?

You're never too old to...

... spend an entire
summer day barefoot.

You're never too old to...

... take up fencing.

You're never too old to...

... count your blessings.

You're never too old to...

... dye your hair pink
and get a tattoo.

You're never too old to...

... go up in a hot air balloon.

You're never too old to...

... be a fashion junkie.

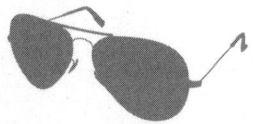

You're never too old to…

… travel first class and treat yourself to lunch in the dining car.

You're never too old to...

... work in a homeless shelter for a day.

You're never too old to...

... design a space rocket.

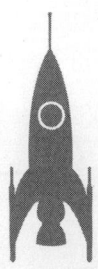

You're never too old to...

... walk down the street bopping your head to the tunes on your MP3 player.

You're never too old to...

... go skinny-dipping.

You're never too old to...

... share a private joke.

You're never too old to...

... eat a Knickerbocker Glory.

You're never too old to...

... learn to meditate.

You're never too old to...

... have a crush on a film star.

You're never too old to...

... climb to the top of St Paul's and admire the view.

You're never too old to...

... write a poem.

You're never too old to...

... wear high heels.

You're never too old to…

… stay in the honeymoon suite of your favourite hotel.

You're never too old to...

... be whisked off your feet.

You're never too old to...

... become a wine buff.
Move over, Hugh Johnson!

You're never too old to...

... sit on Santa's knee.

You're never too old to...

... rock out at Glastonbury.

You're never too old to...

... learn a new language.

You're never too old to...

... try sushi for the first time.

You're never too old to...

... wear a flower in your hair.

You're never too old to...

... discover that you actually *do* like Marmite.

You're never too old to...

... go blonde.

You're never too old to...

... drink a milkshake through a straw and make loud bubbly sounds when you get to the bottom of the glass.

You're never too old to...

... offer to help someone.

You're never too old to...

... build a sandcastle.

You're never too old to...

... be cheeky.

You're never too old to...

... get into a new
style of music.

You're never too old to...

... run that race.

You're never too old to...

... make someone's day.

You're never too old to...

... do a silly walk.

You're never too old to...

... watch the sun rise.

You're never too old to...

... eat something
'naughty but nice'.

You're never too old to…

… get in touch with
an old friend.

You're never too old to...

... send a Valentine's card.

You're never too old to…

… have a flutter on the horses.

You're never too old to...

... kiss someone for
the first time.

You're never too old to...

... climb a tree.

You're never too old to…

… have champagne for breakfast. Buck's Fizz is practically orange juice anyway.

You're never too old to...

... wear fancy dress.

You're never too old to...

... invent a cocktail.

You're never too old to...

... take a gap year.

You're never too old to...

... jump down the last step.

You're never too old to...

... dream about being able to fly.

You're never too old to...

... stay up late watching horror films.

You're never too old to...

... have whipped cream *and* sprinkles.

You're never too old to...

... have a beautiful man or woman on each arm.

You're never too old to...

... go back to school.

You're never too old to...

... turn up the music.

You're never too old to...

... get into recycling.

You're never too old to...

... have a second dinner.

You're never too old to...

... tell a stranger their hat/bag/necklace is fantastic (delete as appropriate).

You're never too old to...

... fall briefly in love with your waiter or waitress.

You're never too old to...

... start the conga line.

You're never too old to...

... slip into something 'more comfortable'.

You're never too old to...

... go on a magical
mystery tour.

You're never too old to...

... sit at the front of the rollercoaster.

You're never too old to...

... perfect the art of toasting marshmallows.

You're never too old to...

... avoid the cracks
in the pavement.

You're never too old to...

... order it shaken, not stirred.

You're never too old to...

... wear a Stetson and have finger-gun shoot-outs.

You're never too old to...

... be at the front of the gig, even if it's in a concert hall, not a stadium.

You're never too old to...

... ask someone to dance.

You're never too old to...

... be King or Queen
of the BBQ.

You're never too old to...

... have a stick-on moustache for ever day of the week. Monday is the 'Selleck'.

You're never too old to...

... pretend to be a waxwork at Madame Tussaud's.

You're never too old to...

... invent the ultimate sandwich. The 'One of Each', anyone?

You're never too old to...

... beat your personal best.

You're never too old to...

... spend several hours planning 'Operation Remote Control'.

You're never too old to...

... have a conker fight.

You're never too old to...

... spend a night in a tepee.

You're never too old to...

... take a ride on a ghost train.

You're never too old to...

... get butterflies in your stomach.

You're never too old to...

... be someone's hero.

You're never too old to...

... enjoy the moment.

You're never too old to...

... make your dreams
come true.

www.summersdale.com